A Literature Kit™ F O R

The Paper Bag Princess

• • • • • • • • • • • • • • • • • •

By Robert N. Munsch

Written by Marie-Helen Goyetche

GRADES 1 - 2

Classroom Complete Press

P.O. Box 19729
San Diego, CA 92159
Tel: 1-800-663-3609 / Fax: 1-800-663-3608
Email: service@classroomcompletepress.com

www.classroomcompletepress.com

ISBN-13: 978-1-55319-320-3
ISBN-10: 1-55319-320-2

© 2007

Permission to Reproduce

Critical Thinking Skills

The Paper Bag Princess

Skills For Critical Thinking		Phonics	Word Study	Comprehension	Reading Response	Writing Tasks	Graphic Organizers
LEVEL 1 Knowledge	• Identify Story Elements			✓		✓	
	• Recall Details	✓	✓	✓	✓		
	• Match			✓			
	• Sequence			✓			
	• List		✓	✓	✓	✓	✓
	• Recognize basic concepts	✓	✓				✓
LEVEL 2 Comprehension	• Recognize Similarities & Differences			✓			
	• Recognize Main Idea			✓			
	• Describe				✓		
	• Classify	✓	✓	✓		✓	
	• Illustrate		✓		✓		
LEVEL 3 Application	• Organize					✓	✓
	• Interview					✓	
	• Make Inferences			✓			
LEVEL 4 Analysis	• Draw Conclusions				✓		
	• Recognize Cause & Effect					✓	
LEVEL 5 Synthesis	• Predict				✓		
	• Imagine Improvements				✓	✓	✓
	• Create					✓	
	• Imagine Alternatives				✓	✓	✓
LEVEL 6 Evaluation	• Ask Questions					✓	
	• Make Judgements				✓	✓	
	• Distinguish between Fact & Fiction						✓

Based on Bloom's Taxonomy

The Paper Bag Princess CC2101

Contents

Assessment Rubric

The Paper Bag Princess

Student's Name: _____ Task: _____ Level:_____

	Level 1	Level 2	Level 3	Level 4
Details	Student can give one detail from the story	Student can give two details from the story	Student can give three details from the story	Student can give four or more details from the story
Characters	Student refers to characters using he or she	Student refers to characters using the boy or the girl	Student refers to characters using names	Student refers to all characters using full names and titles
Information	Student gives incorrect information	Student gives mixed up information	Student gives literal information	Student gives correct information
Questions and Answers	Student cannot answer any teacher questions	Student provides some answers to teacher questions	Student provides correct answers to teacher questions	Student provides thoughtful responses to teacher questions

STRENGTHS:

WEAKNESSES:

NEXT STEPS:

Teacher Guide

Our resource has been created for ease of use by both TEACHERS and STUDENTS alike.

Introduction

This resource provides ready-to-use information and activities for beginning readers. It can be used in any Language Arts program to strengthen children's **reading, writing** and **thinking skills.** You may wish to use our resource on its own, or as part of a larger unit on the stories of Robert Munsch, a unit on fairy tales, etc. It is comprised of interesting and engaging student activities in language, reading comprehension and writing, and can be used effectively for individual, small group or whole class activities.

How Is Our Literature Kit™ Organized?

STUDENT HANDOUTS

Activities in language, reading comprehension and writing (*in the form of reproducible worksheets*) make up the majority of our resource. There are six pages each of PHONICS activities, WORD STUDY activities, COMPREHENSION activities and WRITING tasks. All are either a half-page or full page long. Also provided is a six-page mini-booklet of READING RESPONSE activities. All of these activities contain words and/or phrases from the story which will help the students learn, practice and review important vocabulary words. The writing tasks and reading response mini-book provide opportunities for students to think and write both critically and creatively about the story. It is not expected that all activities will be used, but are provided for variety and flexibility in the unit.

- Also provided are two puzzles, a **word search** and **crossword**. Each of these worksheets can be completed as individual activities or done in pairs.

- Three **Graphic Organizers** are included to help develop students' thinking and writing skills (*see page 6 for suggestions on using the Graphic Organizers*). The **Assessment Rubric** (*page 4*) is a useful tool for evaluating students' responses to many of the activities in our resource. The

Comprehension Quiz (*page 46*) can be used for either a follow-up review or assessment at the completion of the unit.

DISCUSSION QUESTIONS

It is a good idea to introduce a new story to students by preparing them for reading. Using a read-aloud approach, you may wish to open a discussion with the **Before You Read** Discussion Questions (*see page 9*) in the Teacher Guide. Then, read the story out loud. As you are reading, use the **As You Read** questions to engage the students in the story. Once you have completed the read-aloud and the students are familiar with the story, follow-up with the **After You Read** questions. You can present the After You Read questions orally for a continued whole group discussion, or write them on the chalkboard and have students discuss possible answers in small groups and then report back to the class.

PICTURE CUES

Our resource contains three main types of pages, each with a different purpose and use. A Picture Cue at the top of each page shows, at a glance, what the page is for.

🍎 **Teacher Guide**
- Information and tools for the teacher

✏ **Student Handout**
- Reproducible worksheets and activities

EZ✓ **Easy Marking™ Answer Key**
- Answers for student activities

EASY MARKING™ ANSWER KEY

Marking students' worksheets is fast and easy with our **Answer Key**. Answers are listed in columns – just line up the column with its corresponding worksheet, as shown, and see how every question matches up with its answer!

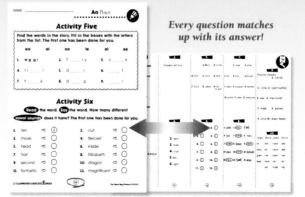

Every question matches up with its answer!

1,2,3
Graphic Organizer Transparencies

The three **Graphic Organizer Transparencies** included in this Literature Kit™ are especially suited to a study of **The Paper Bag Princess**. Below are suggestions for using each organizer in your classroom, or they may be adapted to suit the individual needs of your students. The transparencies can be used on an overhead projector in teacher-led activities, and/or photocopied for use as student worksheets. To evaluate students' responses to any of the organizers, you may wish to use the **Assessment Rubric** (on page 4).

VERBS, VERBS, VERBS

This organizer can be used easily as either an individual activity or whole class **activity. For a class activity,** lead your students in a brainstorming session. Record all the verbs they remember from the story on the board. Students can choose from the following verbs:

> live, marry, smash, burn, carry, put, follow, knock, bang, shout, whisper, eat, sleep, say, fly, breathe, tired, walk

Then, have the children choose six of the verbs from the story and write one verb in each box. They can draw a picture of the verb in the space provided. As an extension activity, have the students write each verb in the past tense. **Found on Page 53.**

FACT – FICTION – WHY?

This graphic organizer will help students develop their reasoning skills and **understand the difference between** fact and fiction. This **can be done as a** class or individual activity. For a class activity, **begin with a discussion in** which students recall things about **the story,** either events that take place, or the **characters themselves.** Write the children's ideas on **the board. Then, have them choose** at least five items **from the list and decide if each is fact** (could happen in **real life) or fiction (make-believe).** They are to write the item **in the corresponding** column of the organizer. For each **point, have the students** give a reason for their answer.
Found on Page 54.

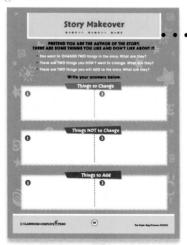

STORY MAKEOVER

For this activity, **the children are asked to take the author's** place. Ask them to **think about how** they would give the story a "makeover". **They are to write** two things that they would change in the story, **two things they would** not change, and two **things they would add** to the story to improve it. They **may wish to change which characters** are in the story, what **the characters are like, what they** say and do, and/or what happens in the story. Encourage the children to be **creative and have fun.** Depending on the writing abilities of **your students, you** may wish to have them write their **answers in complete sentences.**
Found on Page 55.

Bloom's Taxonomy* for Reading Comprehension

The activities in our resource engage and build the full range of thinking skills that are essential for students' reading comprehension. Based on the six levels of thinking in Bloom's Taxonomy, questions are given that challenge students to not only recall what they have read, but move beyond this to understand the text through higher-order thinking. By using higher-order skills of application, analysis, synthesis and evaluation, students become active readers, drawing more meaning from the text, and applying and extending their learning in more sophisticated ways.

This **Literature Kit™**, therefore, is an effective tool for any Language Arts program. Whether it is used in whole or in part, or adapted to meet individual student needs, this resource provides teachers with the important questions to ask, inspiring students' interest, creativity, and promoting meaningful learning.

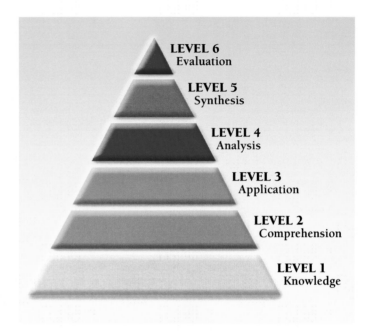

LEVEL 6 Evaluation
LEVEL 5 Synthesis
LEVEL 4 Analysis
LEVEL 3 Application
LEVEL 2 Comprehension
LEVEL 1 Knowledge

BLOOM'S TAXONOMY: 6 LEVELS OF THINKING

Bloom's Taxonomy is a widely used tool by educators for classifying learning objectives, and is based on the work of Benjamin Bloom.

Summary of the Story

The Paper Bag Princess
Story·Robert Munsch   Art·Michael Martchenko
CLASSIC MUNSCH

This is the story of Princess Elizabeth who lives in a castle. Elizabeth is in love with Prince Ronald and they will soon marry. One day, a terrible dragon smashes Elizabeth's castle, burns her clothes and disappears with Prince Ronald! Elizabeth is determined to not let the dragon get away with this, so she decides to go after him. But first, she must find something to wear. Everything is burnt, except for a paper bag. So, clothed in her paper bag, she sets off to follow the dragon's trail (of burnt forests and horses' bones). The trail leads her straight to the dragon's cave and the dragon. Since Elizabeth is very smart, she outwits the dragon by asking him to burn forests with his fiery breath. Two breaths and one hundred and fifty forests later, she challenges him to fly around the world. He shows her how fast he can fly by flying around the world in just ten seconds. Then, she gets him to do it again. This time he does it in twenty seconds. Exhausted by all the activity, he falls fast asleep. Elizabeth steps over the dragon, goes into the cave and rescues Prince Ronald. Unfortunately, he is very upset at Elizabeth because she smells like ashes, her hair is tangled, and she is wearing a dirty paper bag. Astonished by his reaction, she tells him his clothes are pretty and his hair is tidy, but in fact he's a bum. They don't get married after all.

Vocabulary

Included in our Literature Kit™ are 20 vocabulary words from **The Paper Bag Princess** in the form of **word cards** (*pages 43 and 44*). The word cards may be used in a variety of hands-on activities. Also included is a page of 10 blank word cards that may be filled in with other words from the story, or words that fit in with a related subject or theme (*page 45*). You may wish to write the words on the cards or have the children add the words themselves.

Here are suggestions for hands-on activities using the word cards. Make photocopies of the cards for each student or for each group of students.

- Have the children classify the words by parts of speech (verbs, nouns, adjectives, etc.).
- Put the cards face down and have students pick 3 or 4 cards; they can write a story inspired by the cards they select.
- Combine and shuffle the vocabulary words with those from another story (perhaps another book by Robert Munsch, or another fairy tale). Have the children categorize the words by story.
- Have the children use as many word cards as possible to write complete sentences. They will need to write more words on the blank cards (articles, prepositions, etc.)
- Have the children place the words in alphabetical order.
- Have the children work in pairs and each take half of the cards. Without saying the word, one child describes the word on the card, and the other student guesses what the word is.
- Put the cards face down and have students pick up a card and create a word web with it.
- Have the children cut up the words in syllables.

ashes	bum	burnt	carried	castle
dragon	expensive	fantastic	fiery	knocker
magnificent	mess	neat	pretty	prince
princess	tangled	unfortunately	whispered	whole

· · · · · · · · · · Suggestions for Further Reading · · · · · · · · · ·

BOOKS BY ROBERT MUNSCH

The Dark © 1997
From Far Away ©1995
Show and Tell © 1991
Mortimer © 1985
The Boy In the Drawer © 1986
Murmel Murmel Murmel © 1982
Thomas' Snowsuit © 1982
50 Below Zero © 1986
Stephanie's Ponytail © 1996
Wait and See © 1985

Discussion Questions

 Before You Read

1. Why do so many children like stories about princes and princesses?

2. Do you think the story, *Paper Bag Princess* will be a funny story, a sad story, a true story or make-believe?

3. Look at the illustration on the front of the book. What do you think is wrong with the dragon? Is he sick? Tired? Confused?

4. Can you name any other books written by Robert Munsch?

 As You Read

1. If you were Elizabeth and the dragon smashed your castle and took your prince, how would you react?

2. Elizabeth decides to chase the dragon and get Ronald back. What kind of person is she? How would you describe her? What does she have that makes her able to chase a dragon?

3. Since her castle was smashed and the forests burnt, where do you think she got a paper bag?

4. Elizabeth tricks the dragon until he is so tired that he falls asleep. How else could Elizabeth have tried to get rid of the dragon?

5. When Elizabeth goes into the dragon's cave, do you think Prince Ronald will be happy to see her? Why?

6. What do you think the dragon will do when he wakes up?

After You Read 📕

1. What do you think about how Prince Ronald reacted when Elizabeth rescued him from the dragon?

2. When someone does something to help you, how can you show them that you are thankful?

3. Can you recall how Elizabeth outwitted the dragon? Tell the steps in their proper order.

4. Why do you think the dragon was so mean?

5. What part of the story did you like best? Why? Which did you like least? Why?

Robert Munsch

Robert Munsch was born in Pittsburgh, Pennsylvania on June 11, 1945. While he was growing up he had a tough time in school. But he loved to write poetry. He wrote all kinds of poems, even funny ones.

Robert thought he wanted to be a Jesuit Priest when he grew up. He went to university for seven years. Then, he realized that he didn't want to be a priest after all. What he *really* wanted to do was work in daycare!

He loved working with children, and his favorite thing to do was tell stories. He told his stories over and over again without ever writing them down. When he finally decided to write them down, he sent his stories to lots of publishers. One of them said "yes", and that is how he became a published writer.

Today, Robert Munch lives with his family in Canada. He and his wife, Anne, have three children: Julie, Andrew and Tyya. Robert has 50 books published and many stories in the works. Children and adults all over the world like his books so much that they are translated into more than twelve languages! Robert gets many letters and emails from his fans. His biggest inspiration is reading the stories that children send to him.

Did You Know..?

- **Many of his stories are based on Robert's own family.**
- **The year 2005 was the 25th anniversary of *Paper Bag Princess*.**
- **You can write a story and send it to Robert at: Robet Munsch 15 Sharon Place Guelph, Ontario N1H 7V2 Canada.**

Activity One

Circle the word or words that rhyme with the word in the box.

1.	recess	mess	prince	princess	rest
2.	tack	back	whack	whine	sick
3.	snail	snack	stole	real	trail
4.	when	where	ten	again	down
5.	tall	meatball	melt	will	fall

Activity Two

Read the word. Say the word. Which vowel sound does it have? Circle your answers.

1. chase

long a
short a
short e

2. ten

long e
short e
silent e

3. eat

short e
long e
silent e

4. get

short e
long e
silent e

5. yes

silent e
short e
long e

6. cave

long a
short a
short e

Aa Phonics

Activity Three

Here are words from the story. Change the first letter or last letter to make a **new** word.

Examples:

yet ⇨ (n)e t   mat ⇨ m a (d)

1. ten ⇨ ( )e n   2. nose ⇨ ( )o s e

3. bone ⇨ ( )o n e   4. deep ⇨ ( )e e p

5. burn ⇨ ( )u r n   6. can ⇨ c a ( )

7. but ⇨ b u ( )   8. had ⇨ h a ( )

Activity Four

Fill in each blank with the correct word from the story.

1. ⬚ huge / high ⬚ Elizabeth knocked on the_____ door.

2. ⬚ where / wear ⬚ She had to _____ a paper bag.

3. ⬚ nose / toes ⬚ The dragon stuck his _____ out of the cave.

4. ⬚ dizzy / busy ⬚ The dragon told Elizabeth he was very full and very _____.

5. ⬚ tire / fire ⬚ The dragon could breathe a lot of _____.

6. ⬚ rite / right ⬚ Elizabeth put her head _____ inside the dragon's head.

Activity Five

Find the words in the story. Fill in the boxes with the letters from the list. The first one has been done for you.

| ea | ai | oo | ie | ai | ee |

1. w <u>e</u> <u>a</u> r

2. f ___ ___ r y

3. c ___ ___ k

4. t r ___ ___ l

5. d ___ ___ r

6. ___ ___ t

7. t ___ ___ k

8. d ___ ___ p

9. ___ ___ r

Activity Six

Read the word. **Say** the word. How many different **vowel sounds** does it have? The first one has been done for you.

1. ten ⇨ ①

2. out ⇨ ◯

3. move ⇨ ◯

4. fiercest ⇨ ◯

5. head ⇨ ◯

6. inside ⇨ ◯

7. hair ⇨ ◯

8. Elizabeth ⇨ ◯

9. second ⇨ ◯

10. dragon ⇨ ◯

11. fantastic ⇨ ◯

12. magnificent ⇨ ◯

Aa Phonics

Activity Seven

Fill in the blanks with one of these **consonant pairs.**
The first one has been done for you.

| wh | ch | th | sh |

1. Elizabe <u>t</u> <u>h</u>

2. _ _ a s e

3. _ _ o l e

4. _ _ i s

5. _ _ i n g

6. _ _ o u t e d

7. b r e a _ _ _

8. _ _ i s p e r e d

9. b r e a _ _ e d

10. a n o _ _ e r

11. a _ _ e s

12. e v e r y _ _ e r e

Activity Eight

<u>Underline</u> the words that have **short a** sound, like *cat* and *hand*.

(Circle) the words that have **long a** sound, like *bake* and *face*.

Cross out the **a** if it is **silent,** like *boat*.

| Examples: | <u>fast</u> | (ate) | soap |

1. castle

2. stay

3. real

4. had

5. name

6. marry

7. chase

8. dragon

9. paper

10. back

11. came

12. grabbed

13. cave

14. breath

15. ashes

Activity Nine

Write a word from the story that **begins** with each blend. The first one has been done for you.

1. | fl | **fly**

2. tr

3. cl

4. br

5. sl

6. sm

7. str

8. gr

9. pr

10. dr

Activity Ten

Fill in the chart with the words from the list. **Sound out** the words carefully! The first one has been done for you.

~~he~~   end   fell   met   after   add
man   came   piece   tense   paste   rain
red   green   ran   nap   sleep   made

Long e	Short e	Long a	Short a
he			

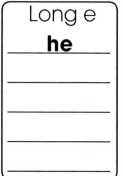
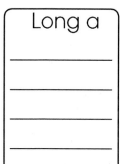

Activity Eleven

1. **Draw** a line from the beginning of the word to the end of the word. **Say** the word. **Write** the word on the line. The first one has been done for you.

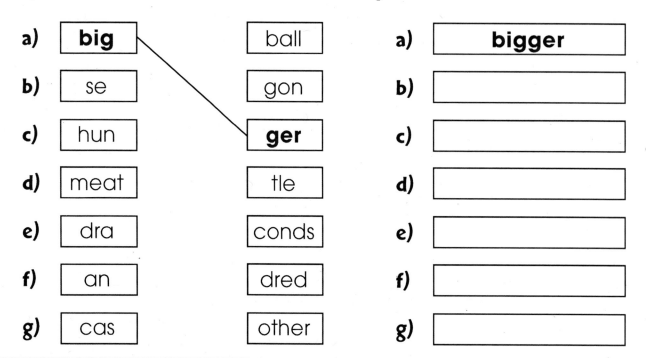

a)	**big**	ball	a)	**bigger**	
b)	se	gon	b)		
c)	hun	**ger**	c)		
d)	meat	tle	d)		
e)	dra	conds	e)		
f)	an	dred	f)		
g)	cas	other	g)		

2. Choose **two** words from the list above. Use each word in a full sentence. Remember to begin your sentence with a **capital letter** and end it with a **period.**

Sentence One

_____

Sentence Two

_____

Activity One

Fill in each blank with the proper **plural noun.**

Use the words in the boxes to help you.

1. | thing | Elizabeth had lost all her _____ because of the dragon.

2. | forest | Elizabeth wanted the dragon to burn ten _____, but at the end he burnt one hundred and fifty.

3. | second | Each flying session took less than ten _____

4. | hair | Elizabeth's_____ was all tangled up.

5. | ash | According to Ronald, Elizabeth smelled like _____.

Activity Two

For each sentence add **quotation marks** **(" ") to show what the speaker says.**

Example: "Oh, yes," said the dragon.

1. Wait, said Elizabeth. Is it true that you are the smartest and fiercest dragon in the whole world?

2. Elizabeth shouted, Fantastic, do it again!

3. Elizabeth whispered, very softly, Hey dragon.

Activity Three

Say the word. Divide the words into **syllables** with a line.

How many syllables does each word have?

1. **to|day**   ⇨ (2)   2. chase   ⇨ ( )

3. carried   ⇨ ( )   4. everywhere   ⇨ ( )

5. banged   ⇨ ( )   6. smashed   ⇨ ( )

7. tomorrow   ⇨ ( )   8. expensive   ⇨ ( )

9. straight   ⇨ ( )   10. unfortunately   ⇨ ( )

Activity Four

These sentences are missing CAPITAL LETTERS. Put in the capital letters where they belong. <u>Underline</u> the lowercase letter and put a capital letter above it, like this:

T   T P   B P
<u>t</u>here is a dragon in <u>t</u>he <u>p</u>aper <u>b</u>ag <u>p</u>rincess.

1. princess elizabeth loves beautiful expensive clothes.

2. prince ronald has never visited new york city.

3. was her castle in europe or in the united states?

4. last year, we visited the grand canyon.

5. my friends and i are on a soccer team called the coyotes.

Activity Five

1. **Busy** is an **adjective** found in **Paper Bag Princess.** It describes the dragon. Find **five** more adjectives from the story. Write them in a list. Be sure to number your list!

Adjectives

_____

_____

_____

_____

_____

2. Write a full sentence using **two** adjectives from your list.

_____

Activity Six

Elizabeth is a name of a character in **Paper Bag Princess.** <u>Underline</u> the words below that are names. ~~Cross out~~ the words that are not names.

<u>Ronald</u>	~~car~~	Simon	box	Alex
princess	toy	food	Robert	head
fish	Michael	castle	bottle	whale
Stephanie	book	Max	zoo	Addison

Activity Seven

Write the words in proper sentence order.

1. marry   Will   or   princess   prince?   a   you

   _____

2. the   dragon?   met   Have   mean   you

   _____

3. didn't   Ronald   married!   get   Elizabeth   and

   _____

4. so   nap.   much,   After   dragon   needed   the   a

   _____

Activity Eight

A full sentence is a complete thought. Are these sentences full sentences? Circle Yes or No.

1. A bright dragon.   Yes   No

2. The dragon listened to Elizabeth.   Yes   No

3. Ronald dragon's owner if   Yes   No

4. Elizabeth was a smart princess!   Yes   No

5. What did Elizabeth do?   Yes   No

6. He flew to.   Yes   No

Activity Nine

The words **large** and **small** are opposites.

Words that are opposites are also called **antonyms.**

1. Find the word from the story that is the antonym for each word below. Use the words in the list to help you. Write the word on the line.

princess   opened   smart   beautiful

tomorrow   whispered   expensive

a) | ugly | _____

b) | prince | _____

c) | cheap | _____

d) | closed | _____

e) | yesterday | _____

f) | shouted | _____

2. Choose **two** antonyms from Question 1 above. Write a **full sentence** using both of the words. Be sure to begin your sentence with a capital letter and end it with a period.

_____

_____

Activity Ten

1. A **noun** is a person, place or thing. Choose **four** nouns from the story. **Write** them on the lines. **Draw** a picture to show what the word means.

a) _____

b) _____

c) _____

d) _____

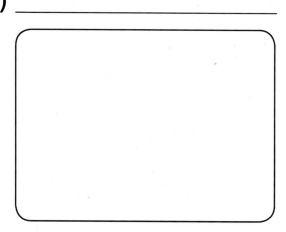

2. Choose **one** noun from Question 1 above. Use it in your own sentence. Write your sentence on the lines. Remember to begin your sentence with a **capital letter** and end it with a **period.**

_____

_____

Activity One

Put a check mark (✓) next to the answer that is correct.

1. **What is this story about?**

   O **A**   a love story between a prince and a princess

   O **B**   capturing a dragon

   O **C**   forest fires

2. **What was the dragon like? He was....**

   O **A**   smart and strong.

   O **B**   a dragon that no one understands.

   O **C**   a show-off who got what he deserved.

3. **What sport did Ronald play?**

   O **A**   He played hockey.

   O **B**   He played soccer.

   O **C**   He played tennis.

4. **What item does Elizabeth take off at the end of the story?**

   O **A**   her rings

   O **B**   her paper bag

   O **C**   her crown

5. **What message is in the story?**

   O **A**   Always look your best.

   O **B**   Be thankful for what you have.

   O **C**   Stay away from dragons.

NAME: _____

Activity Two

T   F   **1.**   Elizabeth was soon to be crowned a Queen.

T   F   **2.**   The dragon wasn't very smart.

T   F   **3.**   Prince Ronald and Princess Elizabeth were married.

T   F   **4.**   The dragon flew around the world twice.

T   F   **5.**   Elizabeth got her paper bag from the grocery store.

T   F   **6.**   Elizabeth needed lots of help to outwit the dragon.

T   F   **7.**   Ronald was grateful to Elizabeth for saving his life.

T   F   **8.**   The dragon burned the castle.

T   F   **9.**   The dragon smashed the forests.

T   F   **10.**   Elizabeth wasn't scared of the dragon.

T   F   **11.**   The dragon flew around the world in ten seconds.

T   F   **12.**   The dragon was dead tired.

 Comprehension

Activity Three

Number the events from ❶ to ❿ in the order they happened in the story.

◯ Elizabeth followed the trail of burnt forests and horses' bones.

◯ After burning one hundred and fifty forests and flying around the world twice, the dragon was exhausted.

◯ Until one day, a dragon smashed her castle down, burnt her clothes and took Ronald.

◯ Ronald wasn't happy to see Elizabeth because of the way she was dressed and the way she looked.

◯ She knocked a second time to ask the dragon if he was the fiercest dragon.

◯ Princess Elizabeth lived in a castle and was going to marry Prince Ronald.

◯ She knocked at the dragon's door.

◯ Princess Elizabeth told Prince Ronald that he was a bum.

◯ Elizabeth arrived at a cave with a huge door and knocker.

◯ All Elizabeth could find to wear was a paper bag.

NAME: _____

Activity Four

Draw a straight line to match the beginning of the sentence to the correct ending.

1 | The dragon wanted to sleep because...

2 | Elizabeth wanted to ask the dragon...

3 | Elizabeth whispered close to the dragon...

4 | Elizabeth wore the paper bag because...

5 | The dragon had no more fiery breath left because...

6 | The trail was easy to find for Elizabeth because...

7 | Elizabeth's castle was smashed because...

8 | Elizabeth put her head in the dragon because...

9 | Ronald told Elizabeth to come back only when...

10 | Elizabeth chased the dragon because she wanted...

she had nothing left to wear. | **A**

she was dressed as a real Princess. | **B**

burnt forest and horses` bones were all over. | **C**

he was exhausted from his travels. | **D**

if he was smart and fiery. | **E**

she wanted to make sure he was asleep. | **F**

the dragon was mean and he wanted to destroy it. | **G**

to catch him and get Ronald back. | **H**

he had just burnt 150 forests. | **I**

she wanted to make sure he was really asleep. | **J**

The Paper Bag Princess CC2101

Activity Five

1 **Fill in the chart below. List <u>five</u> words that describe Elizabeth. List <u>five</u> words that describe the dragon. Remember to number your lists!**

Elizabeth	The Dragon
_____	_____
_____	_____
_____	_____
_____	_____
_____	_____

Are the lists similar? Or are they different? Why?

_____

2 **<u>Underline</u> the words that tell what type of story this is.**

funny   sad   true story   fiction   poem   song

limerick   news   rhyming   nonfiction   haiku   fairy tale

3 **Circle the words that describe where the story takes place.**

in the city   on the beach   in the country   on the river

NAME: _____

Activity Six

**Write the correct word in the box to finish each sentence.
Use the words in the list.**

paper	too	deep	expensive	princess
beautiful	cave	large	fiery	smartest
fiercest	real	old	dirty	whole

1. Elizabeth wore [_____] , [_____] clothes.

2. She put on the [_____] bag and followed the dragon.

3. The dragon was [_____] tired to talk he fell asleep.

4. The dragon took a [_____] , [_____] breath.

5. The [_____] princess lived in a castle.

6. The [_____] door had a [_____] knocker.

7. Elizabeth asked the dragon if he was the [_____] and [_____].

8. Ronald was upset that Elizabeth was wearing a [_____] , [_____] bag.

9. "Come back when you're a [_____] princess!" said Ronald.

10. The dragon ate a [_____] castle that day.

Draw a picture of Ronald.

Look at the picture on the first page of the story (Princess Elizabeth and Prince Ronald). Elizabeth looks like she is in love with Ronald. Does Ronald look like he is in love? How do you think Ronald feels in this picture? What kind of person is he? Write your answers on the lines.

Page One

NAME: _____

Draw a picture of you and the dragon.

Page Two

Elizabeth was very smart when she outwitted the dragon. She tired him out and he fell asleep. What would you have done to outwit the dragon? Write it on the lines below.

Draw a picture of what would have happened to Ronald.

Page Three

What would the dragon have done to Ronald if Elizabeth had not rescued Ronald?

Draw a picture of Elizabeth's new clothes.

Other than a paper bag, what else could have Elizabeth used to cover herself? Write your answers in a list.

Page Four

NAME: _____

Draw a picture of the inside of the dragon's cave.

Page Five

If you could go inside the dragon's cave, what would you find there? What things might be in it? Write it down on the lines.

NAME: _____

Draw a picture of Ronald and Elizabeth together.

Page Six

Prince Ronald was harsh and rude when Elizabeth saved him from the dragon. How could he have behaved in a better way toward Elizabeth? What could he have **said**? What could he have **done**? Tell **why** you think this.

Activity One

Pretend you are a **newspaper reporter.** You will **interview** Princess Elizabeth and Prince Ronald after their ordeal.

Write **five** questions to ask Princess Elizabeth.
Write **five** questions to ask Prince Ronald.

Princess Elizabeth

1 _____ ?

2 _____ ?

3 _____ ?

4 _____ ?

5 _____ ?

Prince Ronald

1 _____ ?

2 _____ ?

3 _____ ?

4 _____ ?

5 _____ ?

Activity Two

A cinquain poem is a simple five-line poem about a person or an object. It follows this pattern:

Line 1	1 or 2 words	(2 to 3 syllables)
Line 2	2 words	(4 syllables)
Line 3	3 words	(6 syllables, can end in *ing*)
Line 4	a phrase	(4 syllables)
Line 5	1 or 2 words	(2 to 3 syllables)

Here is an example:

Pussy cat
Funny, cuddly
Purring, eating, sleeping
Ahh! What a life!
Kitten

Now you try:

Line 1	(1 or 2 words)	_____
Line 2	(2 words)	_____
Line 3	(3 words)	_____
Line 4	(a phrase)	_____
Line 5	(1 or 2 words)	_____

Copy your poem neatly. Draw a picture for your poem.

Activity Three

You love the book, **Paper Bag Princess**, but you don't like the ending. Read the sentences below. Write a new ending by continuing the story.

Elizabeth walked right over the dragon and opened the door to the cave. There was Prince Ronald. He looked at her and said...

_____

_____

_____

_____

_____

Draw a picture for your new ending.

Activity Four

Pretend that you are Elizabeth's personal assistant. You are going shopping for her new clothes. What things will she need? Will she need clothes for warm weather? Cold weather? Will she need new accessories (jewellery) too? Write them in **lists** below. Give each list a **title**.

Title

Title

Title

Title

Activity Five

The dragon feels terrible about the way he acted in the story. From now on he wants to be good. He wants all children to like him. To do this he needs your help!

Write a **code of conduct** for the dragon. List **five** things he must do to be good (Dragon Do's). List **five** things he must not do (Dragon Don'ts).

Dragon Code of Conduct

Dragon Do's

1 _____
2 _____
3 _____
4 _____
5 _____

Dragon Don'ts

1 _____
2 _____
3 _____
4 _____
5 _____

Activity Six

Many of the stories that Robert Munsch writes are stories that children have shared with him. Their stories inspired him to write.

What story could **you** share with Robert Munsch? How could he make your story into a successful book that children all over the world would love to read?

_____

_____

_____

_____

_____

_____

_____

_____

_____

_____

Crossword

Read the clues below. Write the answer where you find the correct number. Be careful! Some words go down. Some words go across.

Across

4. to cost a lot of money

6. messy hair

7. Elizabeth's title

8. beautiful or attractive

10. to wed

Down

1. left over after fire

2. a very big home

3. tidy

5. describes the dragon's breath

9. the day after today

The Paper Bag Princess CC2101

 **Puzzle**

Word Search

1. Find the words in the Word Search puzzle. Circle them.

BAG	BONES	CAVE	DRAGON
FOREST	HAIR	KNOCKER	MEATBALL
PRINCE	WORLD		

M	H	R	K	T	Y	R	B	T	B
G	E	A	O	I	X	E	U	K	A
D	S	A	I	O	P	P	R	N	G
Y	L	S	T	R	D	A	N	O	K
F	T	R	I	B	H	P	X	C	S
S	O	N	O	G	A	R	D	K	E
O	C	R	T	W	E	L	U	E	N
E	B	S	E	G	R	O	L	R	O
S	A	B	U	S	C	A	V	E	B
F	J	H	W	Q	T	R	A	I	L

2. Can you find any words that are (not) in the list above? There are (six!) Circle them in the puzzle. Put them in a (list). Number your list.

_____   _____

_____   _____

_____   _____

The Paper Bag Princess CC2101

Vocabulary Cards

castle	prince
expensive	princess
fiery	burnt
whispered	neat
magnificent	tangled

Vocabulary Cards

ashes	bum
married	pretty
dragon	fantastic
whole	unfortunately
mess	knocker

Vocabulary Cards

NAME: _____

Comprehension Quiz

1. Write the correct word in each blank to finish the sentences.

a) _____ was a beautiful _____.

b) She decided to _____ the dragon and get _____ back.

c) The dragon _____ the castle and _____ the clothes.

d) The dragon flew _____ the _____ twice.

e) Elizabeth and Ronald _____ got _____ after all.

2. Match the item with the character.

tennis racquet	horses' bones	meatball	crown
paper bag	castle	necklace	clothes
crown	fire	cave	knocker

The Dragon

_____

_____

_____

_____

Ronald

_____

_____

_____

_____

Elizabeth

_____

_____

_____

_____

SUBTOTAL: /20

The Paper Bag Princess CC2101

Comprehension Quiz

Answer the questions in full sentences.

3. What is so special about Elizabeth? What made her unhappy?

_____

_____

4. Why did Elizabeth decide to chase the dragon? What did she have to do first?

_____

_____

5. How did she know where to go? Where did this bring her?

_____

_____

6. How did she outwit the dragon? What did the dragon want to do after?

_____

_____

7. Why was Ronald mad at Elizabeth? When could she come back to him?

_____

_____

SUBTOTAL: **/10**

1.
1. mess, princess
2. back, whack
3. trail
4. ten, again
5. meatball, fall

2.
1. long a 2. short e 3. long e
4. short e 5. short e 6. long a

3.
Answers will vary

4.
1. huge
2. wear
3. nose
4. busy
5. fire
6. right

5.
2. fiery 3. cook
4. trail 5. door 6. eat
7. took 8. deep 9. air or ear

6.
2. (1) 3. (1)
4. (2) 5. (1)
6. (2) 7. (1)
8. (4) 9. (2)
10. (2) 11. (3)
12. (4)

7.
2. chase 3. whole
4. this 5. thing 6. shouted
7. breath 8. whispered 9. breathed
10. another 11. ashes 12. everywhere

8.
1. castle 2. (stay) 3. ~~real~~
4. had 5. (name) 6. marry
7. (chase) 8. dragon 9. (paper)
10. back 11. (came) 12. grabbed
13. (cave) 14. ~~breath~~ 15. ashes

9.
Possible answers
2. true, trail
3. clothes 4. breath, breathed
5. sleep 6. smell, smartest
7. straight 8. grabbed
9. prince 10. dragon, dressed

10.

Long e	Short e	Long a	Short a
he	end	came	after
piece	fell	name	add
green	met	paste	man
sleep	tense	rain	ran
	red	made	nap

7.

1. Will you marry a prince or princess?

2. Have you met the mean dragon?

3. Ronald and Elizabeth didn't get married!

4. After so much, the dragon needed a nap.

8.

1. No
2. Yes
3. No
4. Yes
5. Yes
6. No

20

5.

1. Answers will vary
2. Answers will vary

6.

Underline:
Simon Ronald, Alex, Robert, Michael, Stephanie, Max, Addison

Cross out:
car, box, eat, toy, food, head, fish, castle, bottle, whale, book zoo, princess

19

3.

2. 1
3. car/ried 2
4. ev/er/y/where 4
5. 1
6. 1
7. to/mor/row 3
8. ex/pen/sive 3
9. 1
10. un/fort/u/nate/ly 5

4.

1. Princess Elizabeth
2. Prince Ronald, New York City
3. Was, Europe, United States
4. Last, Grand Crayon
5. My, I, Coyotes

18

1.

1. things
2. forests
3. seconds
4. hair
5. ashes

2.

1. "Wait," said Elizabeth. "Is it true that you are the smartest and fiercest dragon in the whole world?"

2. Elizabeth shouted, "Fantastic, do it again!"

3. Elizabeth whispered, very softly, "Hey dragon."

17

11.

1.
b) seconds
c) hundred
d) meatball
e) dragon
f) another
g) castle

2. Answers will vary

16

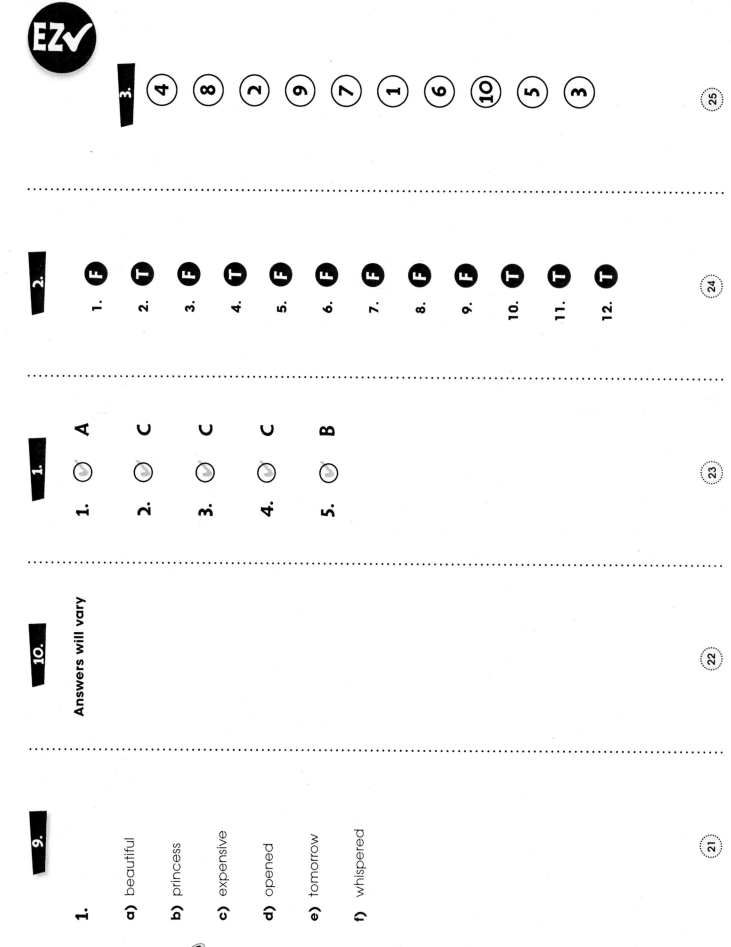

EZ✓

3. ④ ⑧ ② ⑨ ⑦ ① ⑥ ⑩ ⑤ ③

25

2.
1. F
2. T
3. F
4. T
5. F
6. F
7. F
8. F
9. F
10. T
11. T
12. T

24

1.
1. A
2. C
3. C
4. C
5. B

23

10. Answers will vary

22

9.
1.
a) beautiful
b) princess
c) expensive
d) opened
e) tomorrow
f) whispered

21

Across:

4. expensive
6. tangled
7. princess
8. pretty
10. marry

Down:

1. ashes
2. castle
3. neat
5. fiery
9. tomorrow

6.

1. expensive, princess
2. paper
3. too
4. deep, fiery
5. beautiful
6. cave, large
7. smartest, fiercest
8. dirty or old or paper
9. real
10. whole

5.

1. Answers will vary
2. funny, fiction, fairy tale
3. in the country

4.

1. D
2. E
3. F or J
4. A
5. I
6. C
7. G
8. J or F
9. B
10. H

---

29 30 31 32 33 34

Reading Response
All answers will vary

35 36 37 38 39 40

Writing Tasks
All answers will vary

41

28

27

26

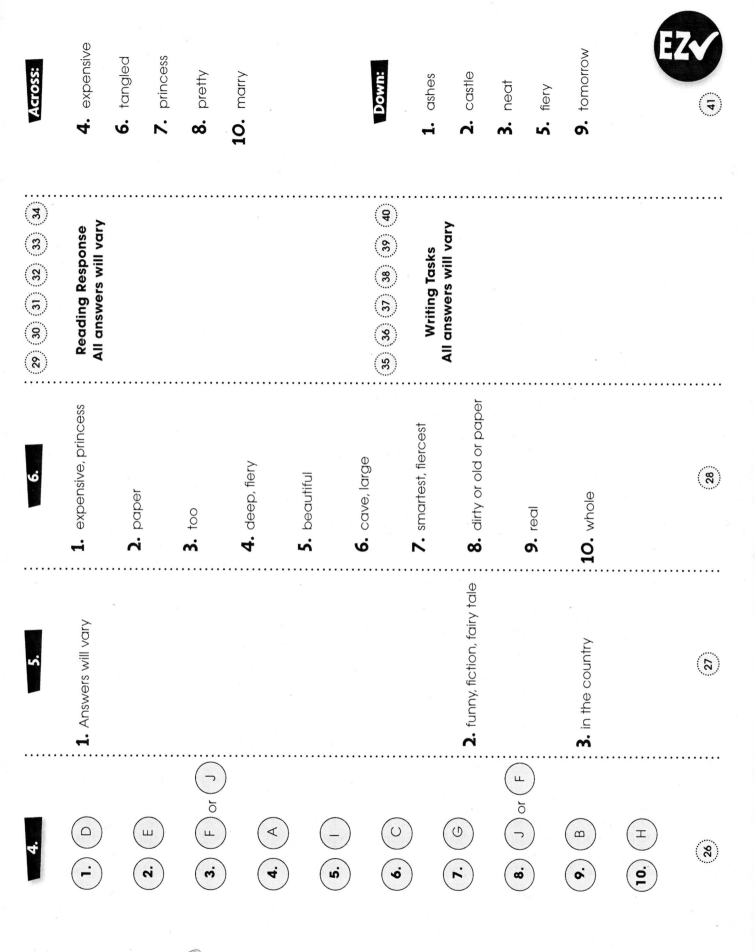

3. She was a princess. The dragon burnt her clothes, smashed her castle and took her prince.

4. She wanted Ronald back. First she need-ed to find something to wear.

5. The trail of burnt forests and horses' bones showed her where to go. The trail brought her straight to the dragons's cave.

6. She made the drag-on breathe out two big breaths of fire and fly around the world twice. Then the dragon only wanted to sleep.

7. He was mad be-cause her hair was tangled, she smelled like ashes, and she looked like a mess. She could go back to see Ronald when she was dressed like a real princess.

1.

a) Elizabeth, princess

b) chase, Ronald

c) smashed, burnt

d) around, world

e) never, married

2.

Dragon:
horses' bones
knocker
fire
meatball
cave

Ronald:
tennis racquet
necklace
crown

Elizabeth:
paper bag
crown
castle
clothes

Word Search Answers

1.

M	H	R	K	T	Y	R	B	T	B
G	E	A	O	I	X	E	U	K	A
D	S	A	I	O	P	R	N	N	G
Y	L	S	T	R	D	A	N	O	K
F	T	R	I	B	H	P	X	C	S
S	O	N	O	G	A	R	D	K	E
O	C	R	T	W	E	L	U	E	N
E	B	S	E	G	R	O	L	R	O
S	A	B	U	S	C	A	V	E	B
F	J	H	W	Q	T	R	A	I	L

2.

fast   burn

paper   trail

huge   door

The Paper Bag Princess CC2101

VERBS, VERBS, VERBS!

●●●●●●●●●●●●●●●

VERBS ARE <u>ACTION</u> WORDS.
THEY TELL WHAT A CHARACTER IS DOING.

- Choose six verbs from the story.
- **Write** one verb in each box.
- Draw a picture for each verb.

1. _____

2. _____

3. _____

4. _____

5. _____

6. _____

FACT - FICTION - WHY?

THINK OF <u>FIVE</u> THINGS THAT HAPPENED IN THE STORY.

- Is each thing <u>fact</u>? (It could happen in real life.)
- Or is it <u>fiction</u> (make-believe)?
- Tell why you think this.

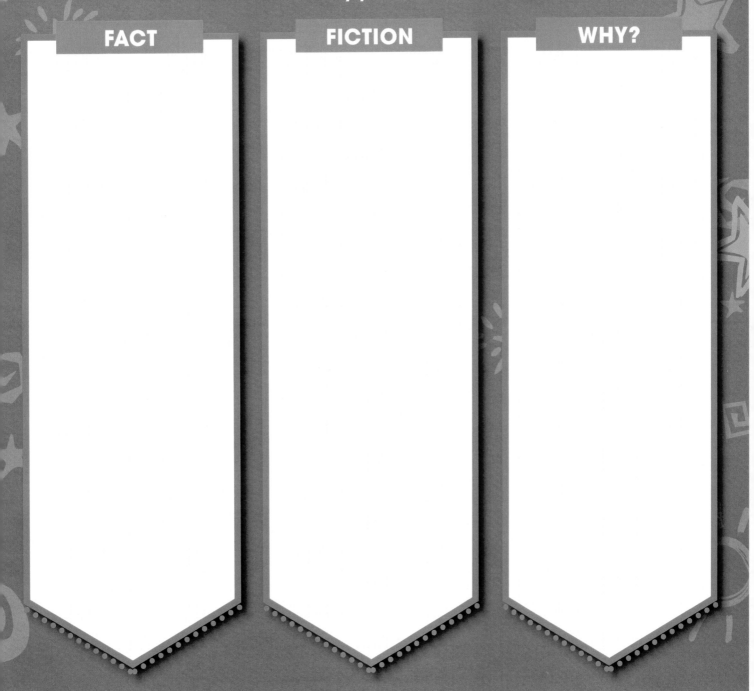

FACT	FICTION	WHY?

Story Makeover

**PRETEND YOU ARE THE AUTHOR OF THE STORY.
THERE ARE SOME THINGS YOU LIKE AND DON'T LIKE ABOUT IT.**

- You want to CHANGE TWO things in the story. What are they?
- There are TWO things you DON'T want to change. What are they?
- There are TWO things you will ADD to the story. What are they?

Write your answers below.

Things to Change

1

2

Things NOT to Change

1

2

Things to Add

1

2

Publication Listing

Ask Your Dealer About Our Complete Line

ENVIRONMENTAL STUDIES

ITEM #	TITLE
	MANAGING OUR WASTE SERIES
CC5764	Waste: At the Source
CC5765	Prevention, Recycling & Conservation
CC5766	Waste: The Global View
CC5767	Waste Management Big Book
	CLIMATE CHANGE SERIES
CC5769	Global Warming: Causes
CC5770	Global Warming: Effects
CC5771	Global Warming: Reduction
CC5772	Global Warming Big Book
	GLOBAL WATER SERIES
CC5773	Conservation: Fresh Water Resources
CC5774	Conservation: Ocean Water Resources
CC5775	Conservation: Waterway Habitats Resources
CC5776	Water Conservation Big Book
	CARBON FOOTPRINT SERIES
CC5778	Reducing Your Own Carbon Footprint
CC5779	Reducing Your School's Carbon Footprint
CC5780	Reducing Your Community's Carbon Footprint
CC5781	Carbon Footprint Big Book

LANGUAGE ARTS

ITEM #	TITLE
	WRITING SKILLS SERIES
CC1100	How to Write a Paragraph
CC1101	How to Write a Book Report
CC1102	How to Write an Essay
CC1103	Master Writing Big Book
	READING SKILLS SERIES
CC1116	Reading Comprehension
CC1117	Literary Devices
CC1118	Critical Thinking
CC1119	Master Reading Big Book

REGULAR & REMEDIAL EDUCATION

Reading Level 3-4 Grades 5-8

SCIENCE

ITEM #	TITLE
	ECOLOGY & THE ENVIRONMENT SERIES
CC4500	Ecosystems
CC4501	Classification & Adaptation
CC4502	Cells
CC4503	Ecology & The Environment Big Book
	MATTER & ENERGY SERIES
CC4504	Properties of Matter
CC4505	Atoms, Molecules & Elements
CC4506	Energy
CC4507	The Nature of Matter Big Book
	FORCE & MOTION SERIES
CC4508	Force
CC4509	Motion
CC4510	Simple Machines
CC4511	Force, Motion & Simple Machines Big Book
	SPACE & BEYOND SERIES
CC4512	Space - Solar Systems
CC4513	Space - Galaxies & The Universe
CC4514	Space - Travel & Technology
CC4515	Space Big Book
	HUMAN BODY SERIES
CC4516	Cells, Skeletal & Muscular Systems
CC4517	Nervous, Senses & Respiratory Systems
CC4518	Circulatory, Digestive & Reproductive Systems
CC4519	Human Body Big Book

SOCIAL STUDIES

ITEM #	TITLE
	NORTH AMERICAN GOVERNMENTS SERIES
CC5757	American Government
CC5758	Canadian Government
CC5759	Mexican Government
CC5760	Governments of North America Big Book
	WORLD GOVERNMENTS SERIES
CC5761	World Political Leaders
CC5762	World Electoral Processes
CC5763	Capitalism vs. Communism
CC5777	World Politics Big Book
	WORLD CONFLICT SERIES
CC5500	American Civil War
CC5511	American Revolutionary War
CC5512	American Wars Big Book
CC5501	World War I
CC5502	World War II
CC5503	World Wars I & II Big Book
CC5505	Korean War
CC5506	Vietnam War
CC5507	Korean & Vietnam Wars Big Book
CC5508	Persian Gulf War (1990-1991)
CC5509	Iraq War (2003-2010)
CC5510	Gulf Wars Big Book
	WORLD CONTINENTS SERIES
CC5750	North America
CC5751	South America
CC5768	The Americas Big Book
CC5752	Europe
CC5753	Africa
CC5754	Asia
CC5755	Australia
CC5756	Antarctica
	WORLD CONNECTIONS SERIES
CC5782	Culture, Society & Globalization
CC5783	Economy & Globalization
CC5784	Technology & Globalization
CC5785	Globalization Big Book
	MAPPING SKILLS SERIES
CC5786	Grades PK-2 Mapping Skills with Google Earth
CC5787	Grades 3-5 Mapping Skills with Google Earth
CC5788	Grades 6-8 Mapping Skills with Google Earth
CC5789	Grades PK-8 Mapping Skills with Google Earth Big Book

VISIT:

www.CLASSROOM COMPLETE PRESS.com

To view sample pages from each book

LITERATURE KITS™ (Novel Study Guides)

ITEM #	TITLE
	GRADES 1-2
CC2100	Curious George (H. A. Rey)
CC2101	Paper Bag Princess (Robert N. Munsch)
CC2102	Stone Soup (Marcia Brown)
CC2103	The Very Hungry Caterpillar (Eric Carle)
CC2104	Where the Wild Things Are (Maurice Sendak)
	GRADES 3-4
CC2300	Babe: The Gallant Pig (Dick King-Smith)
CC2301	Because of Winn-Dixie (Kate DiCamillo)
CC2302	The Tale of Despereaux (Kate DiCamillo)
CC2303	James and the Giant Peach (Roald Dahl)
CC2304	Ramona Quimby, Age 8 (Beverly Cleary)
CC2305	The Mouse and the Motorcycle (Beverly Cleary)
CC2306	Charlotte's Web (E.B. White)
CC2307	Owls in the Family (Farley Mowat)
CC2308	Sarah, Plain and Tall (Patricia MacLachlan)
CC2309	Matilda (Roald Dahl)
CC2310	Charlie & The Chocolate Factory (Roald Dahl)
CC2311	Frindle (Andrew Clements)
CC2312	M.C. Higgins, the Great (Virginia Hamilton)
CC2313	The Family Under The Bridge (N.S. Carlson)
	GRADES 5-6
CC2500	Black Beauty (Anna Sewell)
CC2501	Bridge to Terabithia (Katherine Paterson)
CC2502	Bud, Not Buddy (Christopher Paul Curtis)
CC2503	The Egypt Game (Zilpha Keatley Snyder)
CC2504	The Great Gilly Hopkins (Katherine Paterson)
CC2505	Holes (Louis Sachar)
CC2506	Number the Stars (Lois Lowry)
CC2507	The Sign of the Beaver (E.G. Speare)
CC2508	The Whipping Boy (Sid Fleischman)
CC2509	Island of the Blue Dolphins (Scott O'Dell)
CC2510	Underground to Canada (Barbara Smucker)
CC2511	Loser (Jerry Spinelli)
CC2512	The Higher Power of Lucky (Susan Patron)
CC2513	Kira-Kira (Cynthia Kadohata)
CC2514	Dear Mr. Henshaw (Beverly Cleary)
CC2515	The Summer of the Swans (Betsy Byars)
CC2516	Shiloh (Phyllis Reynolds Naylor)
CC2517	A Single Shard (Linda Sue Park)
CC2518	Hoot (Carl Hiaasen)
CC2519	Hatchet (Gary Paulsen)
CC2520	The Giver (Lois Lowry)
CC2521	The Graveyard Book (Neil Gaiman)
CC2522	The View From Saturday (E.L. Konigsburg)
CC2523	Hattie Big Sky (Kirby Larson)
CC2524	When You Reach Me (Rebecca Stead)
CC2525	Criss Cross (Lynne Rae Perkins)
CC2526	A Year Down Yonder (Richard Peck)
	GRADES 7-8
CC2700	Cheaper by the Dozen (Frank B. Gilbreth)
CC2701	The Miracle Worker (William Gibson)
CC2702	The Red Pony (John Steinbeck)
CC2703	Treasure Island (Robert Louis Stevenson)
CC2704	Romeo & Juliet (William Shakespeare)
CC2705	Crispin: The Cross of Lead (Avi)
	GRADES 9-12
CC2001	To Kill A Mockingbird (Harper Lee)
CC2002	Angela's Ashes (Frank McCourt)
CC2003	The Grapes of Wrath (John Steinbeck)
CC2004	The Good Earth (Pearl S. Buck)
CC2005	The Road (Cormac McCarthy)
CC2006	The Old Man and the Sea (Ernest Hemingway)

REGULAR EDUCATION
● ● ● ● ● ● ● ● ● ● ● ● ● ● ● ● ●

LANGUAGE ARTS

ITEM #	TITLE
	READING RESPONSE FORMS SERIES
CC1106	Reading Response Forms: Grades 1-2
CC1107	Reading Response Forms: Grades 3-4
CC1108	Reading Response Forms: Grades 5-6
CC1109	Reading Response Forms Big Book: Grades 1-6
	WORD FAMILIES SERIES
CC1110	Word Families - Short Vowels: Grades PK-1
CC1111	Word Families - Long Vowels: Grades PK-1
CC1112	Word Families - Vowels Big Book: Grades K-1
	SIGHT & PICTURE WORDS SERIES
CC1113	High Frequency Sight Words: Grades PK-1
CC1114	High Frequency Picture Words: Grades PK-1
CC1115	Sight & Picture Words Big Book Grades PK-1

INTERACTIVE WHITEBOARD SOFTWARE

ITEM #	TITLE
	WORD FAMILIES SERIES
CC7112	Word Families - Short Vowels Grades PK-2
CC7113	Word Families - Long Vowels Grades PK-2
CC7114	Word Families - Vowels Big Box Grades PK-2
	SIGHT & PICTURE WORDS SERIES
CC7100	High Frequency Sight Words Grades PK-2
CC7101	High Frequency Picture Words Grades PK-2
CC7102	Sight & Picture Words Big Box Grades PK-2
	WRITING SKILLS SERIES
CC7104	How to Write a Paragraph Grades 3-8
CC7105	How to Write a Book Report Grades 3-8
CC7106	How to Write an Essay Grades 3-8
CC7107	Master Writing Big Box Grades 3-8
	READING SKILLS SERIES
CC7108	Reading Comprehension Grades 3-8
CC7109	Literary Devices Grades 3-8
CC7110	Critical Thinking Grades 3-8
CC7111	Master Reading Big Box Grades 3-8
	PRINCIPLES & STANDARDS OF MATH SERIES
CC7315	Five Strands of Math Big Box Grades PK-2
CC7316	Five Strands of Math Big Box Grades 3-5
CC7317	Five Strands of Math Big Box Grades 6-8
	SPACE & BEYOND SERIES
CC7557	Solar System Grades 3-8
CC7558	Galaxies & The Universe Grades 3-8
CC7559	Space Travel & Technology Grades 3-8
CC7560	Space Big Box Grades 3-8
	HUMAN BODY SERIES
CC7549	Cells, Skeletal & Muscular Systems Grades 3-8
CC7550	Senses, Nervous & Respiratory Systems Grades 3-8
CC7551	Circulatory, Digestive & Reproductive Systems Grades 3-8
CC7552	Human Body Big Box Grades 3-8
	FORCE, MOTION & SIMPLE MACHINES SERIES
CC7553	Force Grades 3-8
CC7554	Motion Grades 3-8
CC7555	Simple Machines Grades 3-8
CC7556	Force, Motion & Simple Machines Big Box Grades 3-8
	CLIMATE CHANGE SERIES
CC7747	Global Warming: Causes Grades 3-8
CC7748	Global Warming: Effects Grades 3-8
CC7749	Global Warming: Reduction Grades 3-8
CC7750	Global Warming Big Box Grades 3-8

MATHEMATICS

ITEM #	TITLE
	PRINCIPLES & STANDARDS OF MATH SERIES
CC3100	Grades PK-2 Number & Operations Task Sheets
CC3101	Grades PK-2 Algebra Task Sheets
CC3102	Grades PK-2 Geometry Task Sheets
CC3103	Grades PK-2 Measurement Task Sheets
CC3104	Grades PK-2 Data Analysis & Probability Task Sheets
CC3105	Grades PK-2 Five Strands of Math Big Book Task Sheets
CC3106	Grades 3-5 Number & Operations Task Sheets
CC3107	Grades 3-5 Algebra Task Sheets
CC3108	Grades 3-5 Geometry Task Sheets
CC3109	Grades 3-5 Measurement Task Sheets
CC3110	Grades 3-5 Data Analysis & Probability Task Sheets
CC3111	Grades 3-5 Five Strands of Math Big Book Task Sheets
CC3112	Grades 6-8 Number & Operations Task Sheets
CC3113	Grades 6-8 Algebra Task Sheets
CC3114	Grades 6-8 Geometry Task Sheets
CC3115	Grades 6-8 Measurement Task Sheets
CC3116	Grades 6-8 Data Analysis & Probability Task Sheets
CC3117	Grades 6-8 Five Strands of Math Big Book Task Sheets
	PRINCIPLES & STANDARDS OF MATH SERIES
CC3200	Grades PK-2 Number & Operations Drill Sheets
CC3201	Grades PK-2 Algebra Drill Sheets
CC3202	Grades PK-2 Geometry Drill Sheets
CC3203	Grades PK-2 Measurement Drill Sheets
CC3204	Grades PK-2 Data Analysis & Probability Drill Sheets
CC3205	Grades PK-2 Five Strands of Math Big Book Drill Sheets
CC3206	Grades 3-5 Number & Operations Drill Sheets
CC3207	Grades 3-5 Algebra Drill Sheets
CC3208	Grades 3-5 Geometry Drill Sheets
CC3209	Grades 3-5 Measurement Drill Sheets
CC3210	Grades 3-5 Data Analysis & Probability Drill Sheets
CC3211	Grades 3-5 Five Strands of Math Big Book Drill Sheets
CC3212	Grades 6-8 Number & Operations Drill Sheets
CC3213	Grades 6-8 Algebra Drill Sheets
CC3214	Grades 6-8 Geometry Drill Sheets
CC3215	Grades 6-8 Measurement Drill Sheets
CC3216	Grades 6-8 Data Analysis & Probability Drill Sheets
CC3217	Grades 6-8 Five Strands of Math Big Book Drill Sheets
	PRINCIPLES & STANDARDS OF MATH SERIES
CC3300	Grades PK-2 Number & Operations Task & Drill Sheets
CC3301	Grades PK-2 Algebra Task & Drill Sheets
CC3302	Grades PK-2 Geometry Task & Drill Sheets
CC3303	Grades PK-2 Measurement Task & Drill Sheets
CC3304	Grades PK-2 Data Analysis & Probability Task & Drill
CC3306	Grades 3-5 Number & Operations Task & Drill Sheets
CC3307	Grades 3-5 Algebra Task & Drill Sheets
CC3308	Grades 3-5 Geometry Task & Drill Sheets
CC3309	Grades 3-5 Measurement Task & Drill Sheets
CC3310	Grades 3-5 Data Analysis & Probability Task & Drill
CC3312	Grades 6-8 Number & Operations Task & Drill Sheets
CC3313	Grades 6-8 Algebra Task & Drill Sheets
CC3314	Grades 6-8 Geometry Task & Drill Sheets
CC3315	Grades 6-8 Measurement Task & Drill Sheets
CC3316	Grades 6-8 Data Analysis & Probability Task & Drill